A JULIE GIBBS BOOK

for

SIMON & SCHUSTER
AUSTRALIA

Photography by Earl Carter

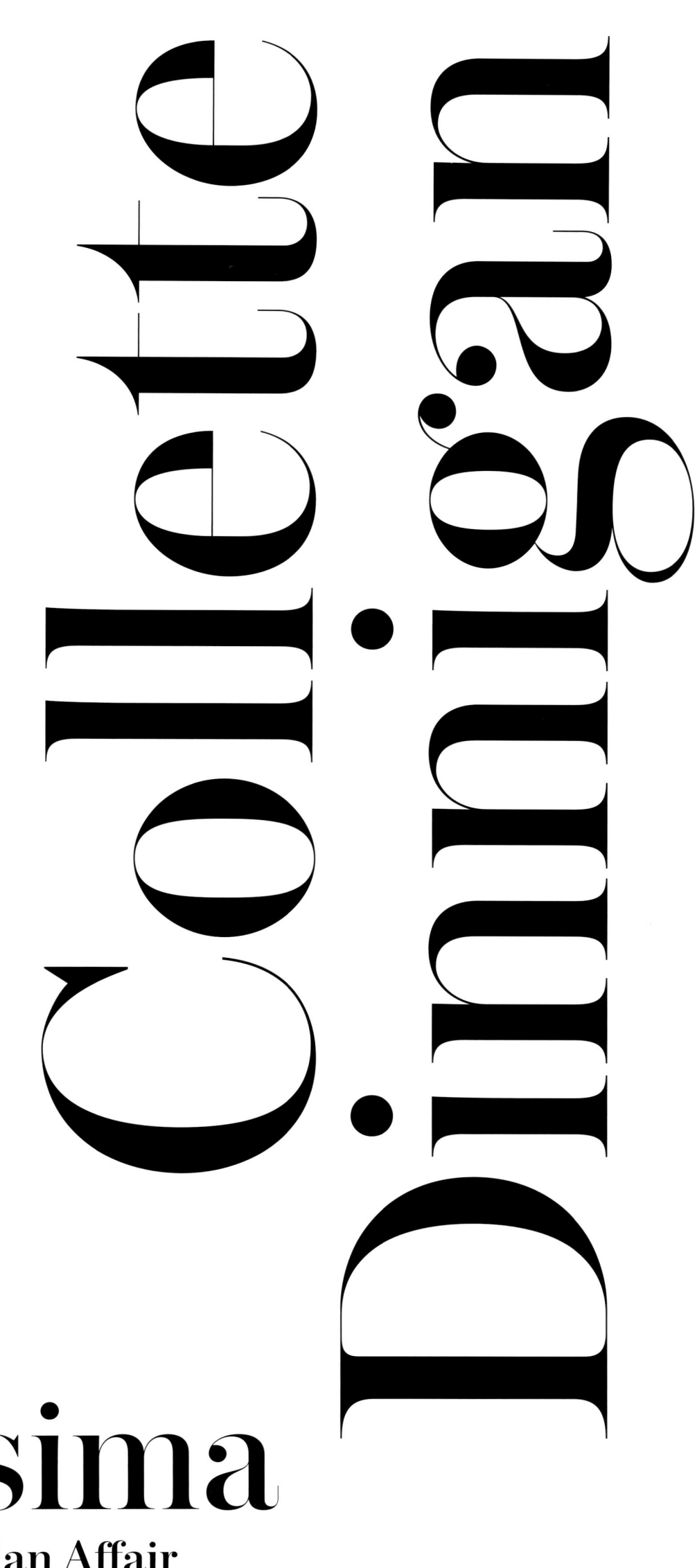

Collette D. Dinnigan

Bellissima

An Australian—Italian Affair

The Great Southern Land [10]

La Dolce Vita [120]

An Australian—

Italian Affair

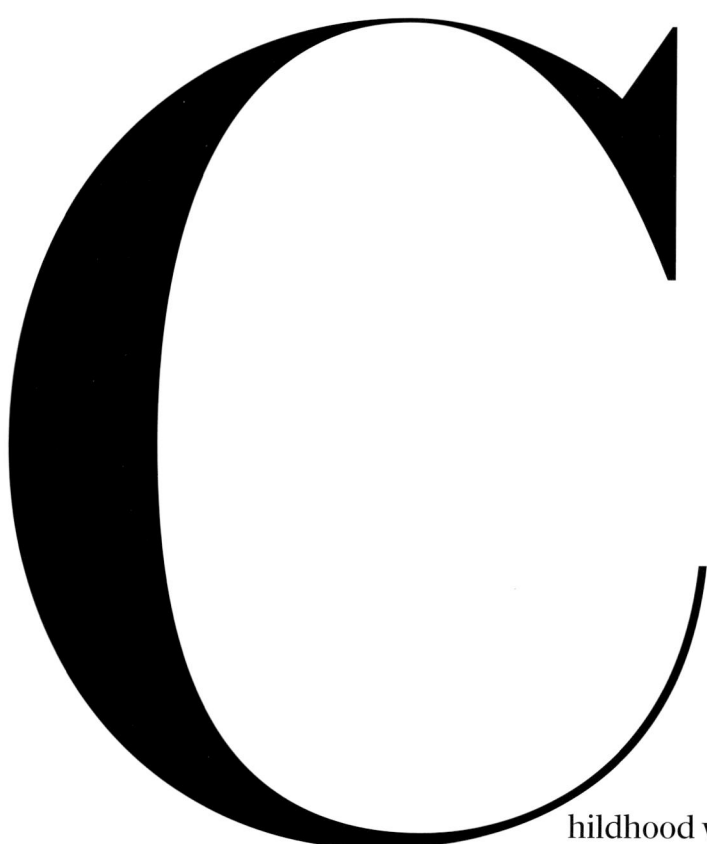

hildhood was fairly unconventional for me, although at the time it seemed perfectly normal. I feel very lucky to have spent so much time with my inspirational parents; an adventurous father (my husband, Bradley, always refers to Dad as 'the last pirate') and an artistic mother. My brother and I were born in South Africa, but we left in the mid-70s when I was about eight and set sail on a world adventure. This early exposure to gathering new experiences ignited a passion for travel that has lingered throughout my life.

I remember Mum would often wake us at night just to see things, whether to admire the beautiful skies filled with shimmering stars or to watch the moonlight hit the phosphorescence on the water, illuminating the waves as if enchanted by fairy dust. Mum saw beauty in everything and she loved to share her wonder at the nuances of nature. It opened my eyes to all the small but exquisite details around us; from how light shifts and stretches throughout the day, to the shapes of blossoms and the palette of a landscape – be it dusty-green eucalypts against an intensely blue sky or the soft sage of an olive grove contrasted with white-washed buildings.

After arriving in New Zealand, we started to build our home. Mum would plant the most beautiful flower beds and scattered throughout would be lettuces, radishes and herbs. Not at all formal in its organisation, rather, it was a gentle chaos. She also made cooking seem effortless and played what she called 'honky tonk' piano, but it was always with passion and good rhythm. Our home in New Zealand, just as our home in Africa, was filled with collectables, art, homemade ceramics, tribal gifts, music, friends and love.

Mum has handed this connection to me and I share her lifelong devotion to home, art, textiles, curiosities, travel, food and, of course, family and friends. These threads are woven throughout my homes in Australia, as well as in Italy, and this book is a collection of those loves. It's an ode to all the magnificent vignettes that colour life, from windswept beach campfires to the joy of an overflowing market basket, teaching the family that food can be medicine, a perfectly placed chair and an exquisite cloth. All made meaningful by enjoying those simple pleasures with those we love most.

Mum was also partly responsible for my 30-year career in fashion. She was a fabric buyer and designed textiles for a boutique in New Zealand. I was lucky enough to get all the remnants, samples and old Butterick patterns (usually all in the larger sizes). By age 12, I was cutting down the patterns and sewing my own clothes.

I could not have wished for a better life in fashion than the one I created. But I still always collected ceramics and textiles, and travelled the world scouring markets for treasures, such as old buttons and lace, as well as various ideas that would influence my collections. Visual beauty and delight in the unexpected was instilled in me by my mother. It was the rocket fuel that propelled my fashion career and now I use the same deep well of inspiration when I decorate homes.

My heart was always in textiles, colour and proportion, so when I left the clothing world behind, it was less of a conscious decision and more of a shift in focus. Following the whims of my creative spirit, I've wandered into a world of handmade ceramics, table linen and home fragrance all inspired by my time in Italy.

Home, wherever it is, is filled with relics from the places I have travelled and the adventures I've enjoyed along the way. I'm always hunting for that which I have not yet discovered. I relish learning the crafts of local artisans, whether it's throwing a vase or making orecchiette by hand, and I can't resist gathering bits here and there that take my eye – just as a bowerbird would.

Sometimes I wonder what will happen to everything when I go. I do feel that I have curated my own little museum of curiosities and collectables that may not necessarily mean anything to others, but for me, each piece tells a story. It might be a $10 oil painting from the markets in Brussels or a more exclusive sculpture from Monaco, but they all sit together in a world that brings me enormous joy.

In the same way as my objective in designing clothes was to make women feel confident and effortlessly stylish, I seek to create homes that have an easy elegance. There's an Italian word, 'sprezzatura,' that so beautifully embodies this concept. It essentially means a studied nonchalance or something that looks to be perfectly graceful, yet easily achieved. Style shouldn't feel overly contrived and I find when you mix pieces, which have an emotional connection, rather than a financial one, your space naturally becomes an expression of yourself. I'm not a trained interior designer, what I do comes from instinct.

For me, interior styling is looking at a space and seeing what's possible, more than it is about working to a formula. Curating spaces is a joyful experience, especially when shared with friends and artists. In these pages you'll meet some of the people with whom I collaborate and have found a profound connection with, be it over a love of where we live, how we eat or art we admire.

No matter whether we are in Italy or Australia, it's important to feel welcomed, sit together at the table, eat wonderful food and talk about things. I hope this book will inspire you to create the same sense of sprezzatura in your home.

The Great Southern Land

Australia

I acknowledge the Traditional Owners of Country throughout Australia. I pay my respects to Elders past, present and future and recognise their continuous connection to Country.

ustralia, the great
southern land. Bold, bright and adventurous. While it wasn't always my home, after
many years running a business and raising a family here, this enrapturing, vivacious
country has a firm hold on my heart.

Australia is a sensory overload that never fails to lift my spirits. It's the chorus of
cicadas, crickets, melodic frogs, the laughing kookaburra and those crazy cockatoos.
It's the sound of rain beating on a tin roof in a wild storm, then after, as the sun
emerges, it's the scent of eucalyptus and the unique petrichor of Australian terroir.
These soul-awakening moments keep me grounded here.

Australia is also a continent of amazing geography, from the spectacular
coastline that meets the often-dramatic shoreline, where gum trees dominate, to the
red earth that blisters in contrast to the big, blue sky that seems to stretch to eternity.
The sun, ocean and elements all beat down with unyielding power – giving the
country a rawness unlike anywhere else I've encountered in the world.

The vibrant communities, towns and cities that fringe and frame this massive
landscape offer their own particular richness. There is so much to be discovered
in this continent of extreme and wild beauty. It can be cruel to those lost in its vast
space, but mostly, I am in awe of its endearing unruliness, unique wildlife and the
endlessly rolling ocean. You can feel wonderfully isolated here, yet still only be an
hour or two from a major city.

There is something exceptional about the Australian light, too. It can be harsh
and yet it's forgiving. The shadows it casts are strong and defined; it's the antithesis
to the filtered luminosity found in Europe, but I find it just as captivating.

Astonishingly, this land has been inhabited by its first people for more than
65,000 years. Interwoven with their ancient lore and living knowledge, Australia
has a youthfulness that comes from generations of immigration, many from Italy.
Perhaps that's why, for me at least, Australia and Italy have an easy synergy.

Because Australian culture feels so comparatively young and untethered from Europe and America, you can have such fun experimenting – you're not judged by the world beyond. You can discover, play and create here, then take it to the world. It always felt a bit undiscovered to me. When I was in fashion, I found its remoteness gave me a confidence to play without restraint.

There's also a comfortability in Australia. I think that no matter what it is, we can work it out. It's wonderful to be able to retreat here, to cocoon and emerge new. I particularly find this at my home in Bowral. I call it 'the commune', as friends come and go, warming it with a wonderful energy. The property is deeply enchanting and I have spent years planting and reseeding the flower beds, so no matter the time of year, we nearly always have cut flowers in the home.

Chickens spend their days grazing happily through a paddock, producing a healthy nest of eggs, which we use to make Neil's Margaret frittata (page 116) and I devote a lot of time to my vegetable patch, which we mostly try to live off, so our menus are unavoidably seasonal.

This brings me to the kitchen – there is always a party here. Everyone is involved in the cooking process, it's a real collaboration. As you'll see in this book, I love to celebrate and cook together. I also love to set the table, whether it's for an impromptu dinner or a more formal occasion. I always have candles, dripping their dark-red wax like lava down the candlesticks, which creates its own dramatic art. I pick roses with their petals falling and use handmade ceramics, antique silver cutlery, napkins from French markets and so on. Illuminated by beautifully dappled and forgiving light, it all makes for a deeply romantic and welcoming table setting.

I truly relish the country calm I find in the Southern Highlands. I know when my children grow older, they will always find their space here and, with it, great memories. It's where they call home.

On the other hand, Sydney life provides a shimmering contrast to the country. I love seeing the lights of the city skyline and the busy harbour full of boats jostling in and out. It's a place that is also very much our home, but it feels more grown-up and perhaps a bit more formal than Bowral.

On the following pages are Australian homes I've created and cherished, from Bowral and Darling Point to the dreamy coastal Rosedale home I loved, but ultimately had to let go when it no longer made sense to our family life.

All these places have been filled with loved ones, good food cooked from the heart, flowers grown in the garden, and art I've collected along the path of my life – whether it's my son's or a John Olsen. In these pages you'll also find recipes and meet some of my dear friends, such as Louise Olsen and Neil Perry. There are also moments from one of my favourite places in all of Australia, Broughton Island. An easily accessible but wonderfully untamed and undeveloped paradise off the south coast of New South Wales, where you can catch your dinner and grill it over coals right there on the pristine beach.

Whether you cook one of the recipes shared here, feel inspired to plant new seeds, grow herbs in a pot on your windowsill where the light slips in so pleasingly, or simply rearrange some furniture and fill a vase with flowers, I hope you find something within these pages that resonates with you.

My love for Broughton Island, which lies 14 kilometres off Port Stephens, exists in tandem with my love for my dear, generous, ocean-loving friends, Ian Puckeridge and his daughter, Lara. For many years we have spent time together on Australia's coastline, whether fishing or diving for lobster and abalone. No matter where we are, I feel compelled to make a beautiful space for us to share a meal. So with us comes everything from copper pots to baskets and linens for our makeshift camp kitchen. Broughton Island is a true adventureland – it's wild, windswept and everything I adore about Australia's rugged beauty.

Broughton Island

Opposite: Ian's daughter, Lara, has followed in his footsteps to become a champion spearfisher, along with her brother, Aaron.

Previous spread: There's no electricity on Broughton Island and you need to bring everything with you. I can't help adding a few aesthetic touches.
Opposite: Ian Puckeridge with a catch of abalone and lobsters, ready to clean.

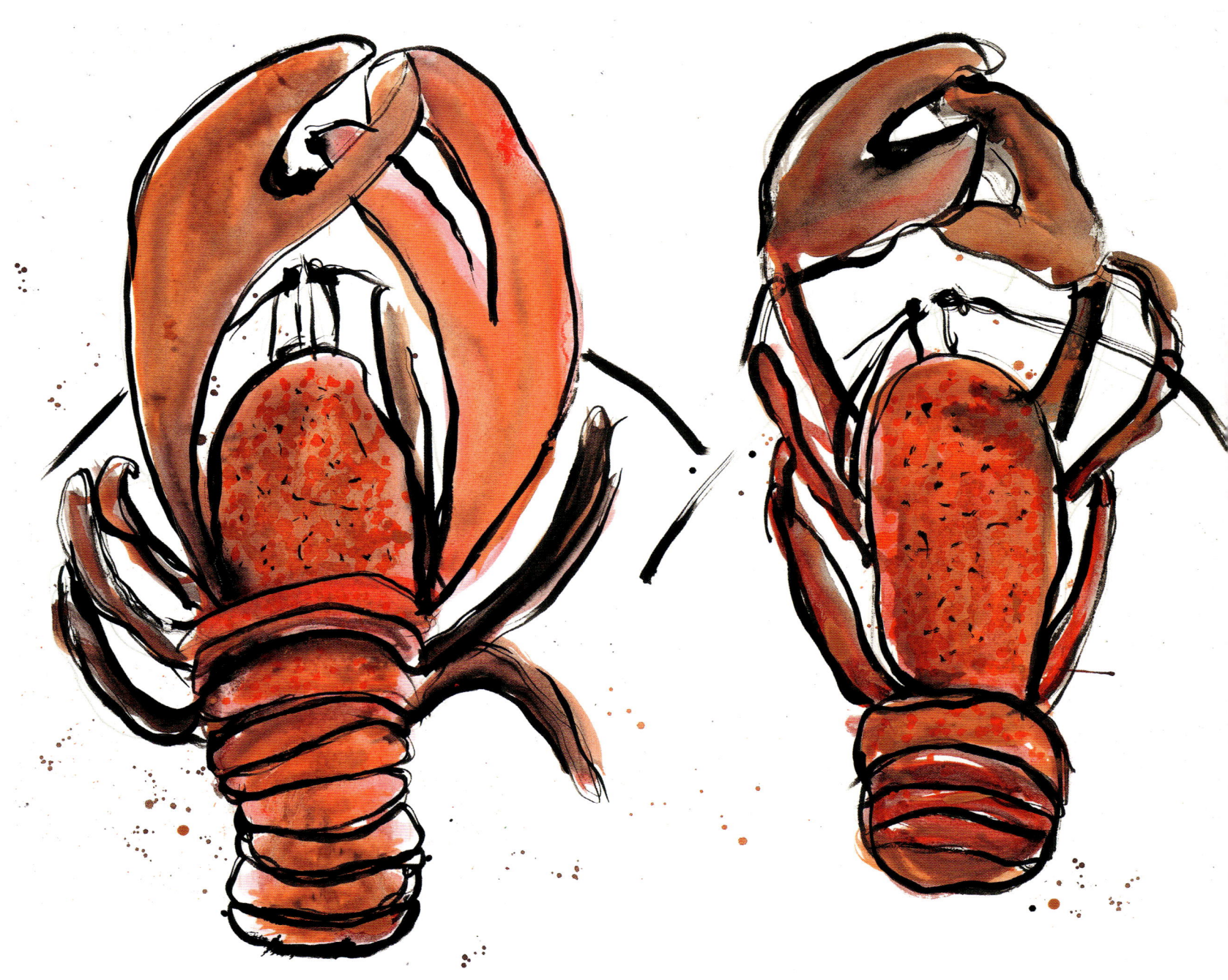

Ocean-fresh abalone needs to be cooked as simply as possible, just tossed on the barbecue with very few embellishments.

BBQ Abalone & Lobster with chilli and garlic

Mix some soft salted butter with chopped garlic & chilli.

Take freshly caught tenderised Abalone and cut them into pieces.

Cover with the chilli butter and cook on the BBQ for a couple of minutes. Cut the Lobsters in half and spread with Butter & Chilli

Cook on the BBQ just until the flesh turns white

Top with chopped parsley and serve with Lemon Wedges

BBQ Whiting

Take your fresh scaled & gutted whiting and place thin slices of lemons, chopped parsley salt & pepper into the cavity

Cook on the BBQ for a couple of minutes on each side.

Serve anointed with olive oil & salt

Garnish with Lemon Wedges and

Offer a Salad of Mustard Greens & Radicchio.

Opposite: I feel this beautifully fresh fish is perfect served on this stainless-steel dish that was handmade by my father.
Following spread: I'm keen to give my son, Hunter, a taste of the adventure I had as a child and Australia is an incredible place for that.

Eurobodalla

I always wanted a place by the ocean. Watching the storms roll in from the balcony
of our Rosedale home, you can feel the energy in the air – it's like a portal to another world.
The whales travel up and down the coast and you can see dolphins surfing the waves.
Each day brings a new narrative of oceanic wonder. After our original and wonderfully
laidback surf shack here burnt down, we had to rebuild to a BAL 40 fire rating, which
presented many challenges. But the result was a much more modern aesthetic and a house
that is also 98 per cent off-grid.

Rosedale

Opposite: From the courtyard you can glimpse the ocean. The warm, handmade Spanish terracotta tiles contrast so well against that brilliant blue.
Above: My husband, Bradley, and my son, Hunter, on the beach outside our Rosedale house.

The beach house has a minimalist aesthetic with a subtle ode to Africa. This Marisa Purcell painting brings in a soft pop of colour.

Our house backs onto a pristine and secluded bay in North Rosedale.

Hill End

Since meeting at one of John Olsen's birthday celebrations, Luke and I have become close friends. We're very like-minded creatively and have collaborated on a children's book together, *Santa loves Australia*. It's always very engaging to be with Luke, he is a positive force of nature who loves to cook, paint, entertain and celebrate life in every way possible. He makes life exciting and his passion for the Australian landscape is evident in his painting. His mentors throughout his career have included the likes of Drysdale, Olley, Whiteley, and Cummings.

Luke Sciberras

Opposite: Watching Luke sketch the cuttlefish for his risotto recipe is mesmerising and a lovely homage to the fish.

Scibbo's Cuttlefish Risotto

Slice & dice the cuttlefish (500g) and their tentacles then saute in a very hot pan with lots of olive oil only for a couple of minutes Add two cloves of garlic chopped finely

When the garlic is softened add 400g of Arborio rice & two shallots finely chopped

After a couple of minutes of gentle stirring add a of white wine simmer briefly & then begin adding hot fish stock one cup at a time

After 15 minutes or so put in two tablespoons of Squid Ink

Season to taste & add a small handful of grated Parmesan

Just before Serving gently fold in about 50g of butter

(On serving add a flourish of Olive oil Red chilli (seeds removed) and Parsley

Southern Highlands

My home in the Southern Highlands is an enchanting and happy place. I immediately fell in love with this old, rabbit warren of a homestead, which was built in the 1890s and had been gifted to the governor general. It took nearly four years to renovate, during which time I was often in Europe sourcing materials and special pieces that would feel at home within the walls of this historic house. It's usually full of people and life and is absolutely brimming with art I've collected over the years. It's inviting, friendly and private, and feels secure and cloistered from the world beyond. There's a magical cottage garden with all manner of fruit trees, vegetables and blossoms, where I spend much of my time, and my studio is also on site. It's a true sanctuary, where I can escape and create.

Bowral

Previous spread: We restored four of these lovely original chimney stacks marked with the homestead's insignia, but we had to replace the roof and window sashes.

Previous spread: When I found these old Egyptian shutters, I knew they were destined for the pool house. The trellis is festooned in purple wisteria come spring.
Above: The internal courtyard of the house is one of my favourite vignettes, especially when the star jasmine is in bloom.

Previous spread: These incredible, 1000-year-old marble tiles in the conservatory were salvaged from an old church in Belgium.
Above: Every bit of wall space is arranged with artwork from my friends and family.

Opposite: I've come to embrace red for a pop of colour. I've used it in the family room here to complement the monochrome Nina Fuga artworks.

Above: The artwork in this room is by a local Southern Highland's artist Jenny Lavender who works with x-ray film.
Opposite: I collaborated with Canadian artist Shelagh Keeley for these artworks that adorn the hallway.

Previous spread: I find this large Schumacher print of Paris in our formal sitting room endlessly fascinating – it totally draws you in.
Above: I found these ancient vessels at an antiques market in Puglia. The age of things you can unearth at European markets always fascinates me.

I love Australian artist Guy Maestri's work; particularly this oil painting called *No Man's Land*, and this modern-looking lamp is actually vintage Murano glass.

Previous spread: The Southern Highlands landscape has my heart. This view of the Robertson Escarpment is one of the most breathtaking in the region.
Above: Guy Maestri's painting 'Portrait of a threatened species' presides over our dining table, set with Collette Dinnigan table linen, napery and ceramics, and garden blooms.

I have a soft spot for this antique clock, which was owned by my grandfather.

The kitchen is the heart of any home. So I love it to feel welcoming and abundant with flowers and fruit picked from the garden.

Broad bean Bruschetta

These are best with soft creamy goat cheese
I use Meredith Dairy Marinated Goats cheese
and their log of fresh Chèvre.

100g jar of preserved soft goats cheese, in oil
80g fresh chèvre, crumbled
1kg broad beans still in their pods
1 Baguette / ficelle
Extra Virgin Olive Oil
8 sprigs of thyme leaves removed from stalks
Pepper

Pod the beans and cook them in boiling water
for 3 minutes
Drain, and as they are cooling,
slip them out of their skins. Roughly
Mash with a fork. Toast slices of the
Bread and drizzle them with oil
Layer each slice with 2/3 feta
and 1/3 Chèvre & then
broad beans Garnish with Thyme Leaves
flowers and ground
Pepper.

Roast Chicken

1 x 1.8 kg Chicken
6 potatoes peeled and cut in half
4 tbsp of soft butter
Half preserved Lemon pulp set aside & skin finely chopped
1 Clove garlic, chopped finely
2 tbsp of chopped herbs — a mix of thyme, rosemary or parsley oregano, sage
1 lemon sliced in half
2 leeks chopped into 1cm slices, 3 spring onions
1 Loaf of Sour Dough Bread
1 Lemon, Extra Virgin Olive Oil, Salt & Pepper

Preheat the oven to 220°C Parboil the Potatoes
Put the butter in a bowl with the preserved lemon, garlic & herbs and mix together. In the cavity of the chicken sprinkle some salt and add the lemon halves.
Loosen the skin of the chicken & put the herb butter under the skin. Rub the skin with olive oil and pepper and then smear the preserved lemon on top.
Spread a layer of olive oil on the base of a large Baking Dish. Arrange large thick pieces of bread to support the chicken on top. Around the edge put the potatoes leeks spring onions and drizzle on more olive oil.

My creative studio is set away from the house; it's my haven, where I can work on multiple projects at once. I'm always collecting fabrics.

My mood board is always changing, depending on what I'm working on. But one thing that never changes is Riley at my feet.

Glenquarry

Louise Olsen and I share a love of the country, seasons and escapism. With Louise being the creative director of Dinosaur Designs, when I was in fashion we often met at various events, but it's really been in the Southern Highlands that our friendship has flourished. We have these very worldly catch-ups in a very country setting – it's wonderful. She is one of Australia's most talented contemporary artists and those few who have been to her studio in the Highlands would agree it's a special place.

Louise Olsen

Opposite: Louise's painting 'Vibrations' together with two Dinosaur Designs side tables.

Aïoli

This is one of the first recipes my father
John Olsen taught me. It's a recipe that
depends on a certain amount of feeling
So adjust the seasoning to taste.

2 cloves of garlic
2 large free range egg yolks
1 cup Extra Virgin Olive Oil
Salt & Pepper
Lemon Juice to taste

Gently crush the garlic with some salt in
a mortar and pestle. Mix in the egg yolks
and, bit by bit, add the olive oil. Once
the mixture starts to thicken, slowly add
lemon juice, tasting all the while, and
whisk thoroughly. Season with Salt & Pepper.

Previous spread: Visiting Louise at her studio in the Southern Highlands is a true pleasure.

Sydney

I've lived in Sydney for many years and have spent the last few renovating our house in Darling Point. Compared to the Southern Highlands, it's a much more grown-up and controlled environment. There isn't the freedom the land gives you, but we have an amazing view over Rushcutters Bay, where you can be a voyeur to the busy harbour beyond. In any city in the world, even Rome, you live in your neighbourhood and here I enjoy a very local existence. It's a lovely contrast to country life, yet I can't help bringing some elements of our rural home to the city with us, such as flowers and produce from the garden, which have a way of softening the formal ambience here. I love how this house is filled with beautiful light that brightens spaces and throws soft shadows and contrast.

Darling Point

I moved this French fireplace to the other side of the room. It was an undertaking, but felt like the right thing to do.

This artwork by Indigenous artist Stewart Hoosen caught my attention the moment I saw it.

Hunter taking a dive in the pool. The reflection of the palm trees in this photo reminds me of Miami or Malibu.

Previous spread: We're often out-and-about when we're in the city, so I wanted to make the house into a calm sanctuary from the hustle beyond the walls. 'Nude V' by Robert Malhope hangs above the fireplace. (From left: Estella, Hunter, Bradley, and Collette)

Opposite: Our Sydney home feels like a tropical oasis with the swaying palms, sounds of halyards clinking in the bay and the wonderfully raucous Australian birdlife.
Above: You don't often see a curve on a pool; we spent a lot of time working with different materials to get it right.

Above: Hunter's room looks over Elizabeth Bay and across to the city skyline. He loves city life, so it's perfect for him.
Opposite: Estella sits in front of Guy Maestri's painting 'Deep Sea Blues'.

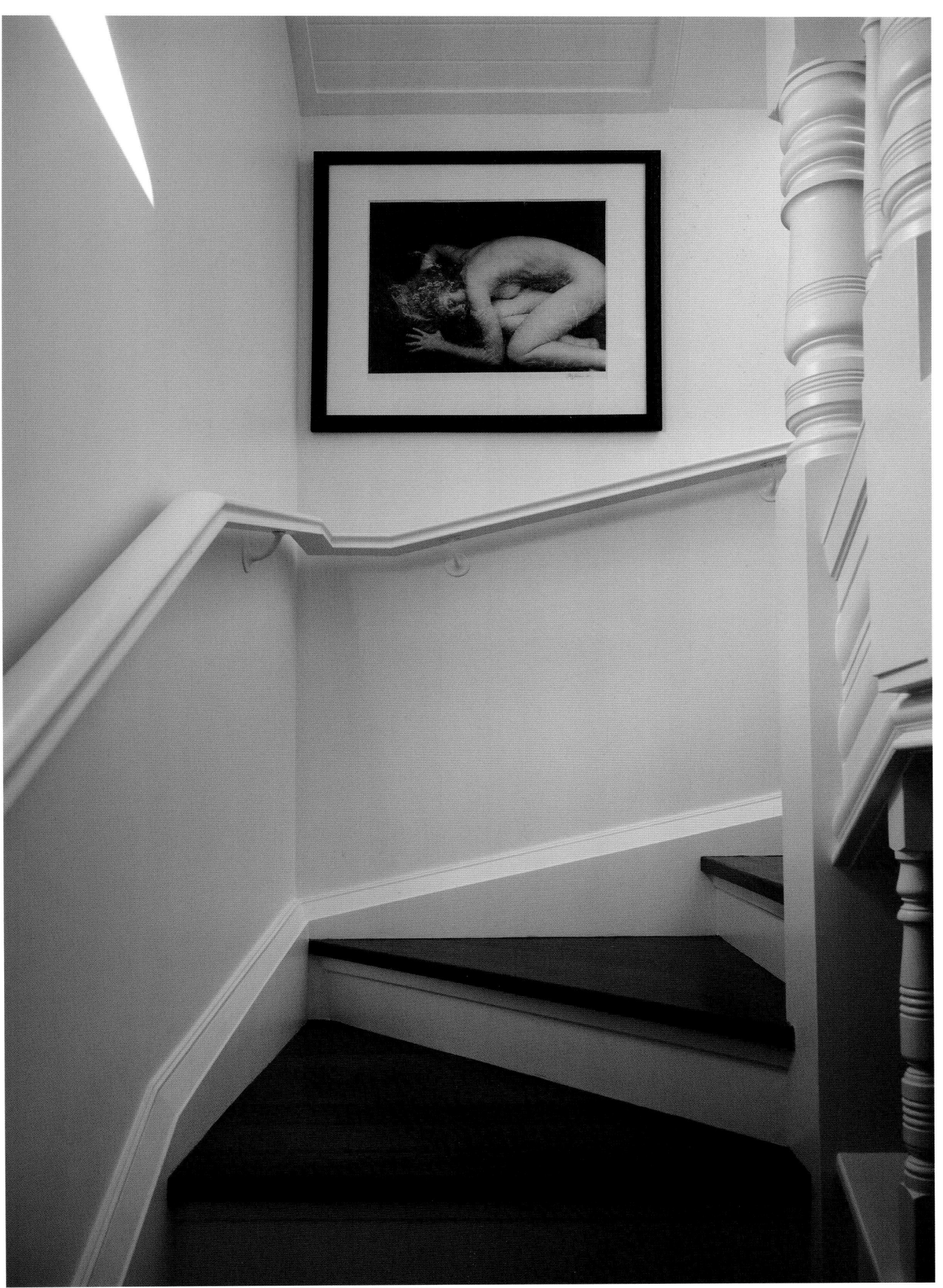

Above: A photograph by Sally Bierman hangs in the stairwell.
Previous spread: This old table has moved everywhere with me. It's from a Danish cheese factory, where they used to sort cheese on top of it.

Above: I keep my bedrooms minimal. I don't spend much time in there, but I love to wake up with sunlight streaming in. The painting is by Robert Malherbe, 'Woman sleeping'.
Opposite: Hanging above a reading corner is a painting by Alan Jones, 'Danningham Reserve'.

My city office is where you'll find me taking Zoom meetings. I try to keep it ordered, but ultimately, an organised chaos takes over.

Sydney

Neil and I have been friends for nearly 40 years. He cooked at some of my first shows in Paris and we had an enormous amount of attention because of it. As Australians, we're so optimistic and we go into everything with our eyes and arms wide open. We embrace the moment and we deliver. I love Neil's ethos when it comes to the kitchen. He's so passionate about food, his suppliers and the environment. He has such an enormous generosity of spirit and uses the best ingredients to cook beautifully considered dishes. And while he is one of Australia's most revered chefs, not everything he cooks is complicated. He also loves simple dishes, such as this frittata recipe he calls 'Collette's eggs', which are from my hens in the Highlands.

Neil Perry

Margaret frittata

5 eggs
1 tbspn Butter
2 tbsp of extra Virgin Olive
oil
3 tbsp soft goat cheese
broken up
Herbs of your choice to put on top EG:
Chives, Dill, Parsley...Salt & Pepper

Crack the eggs into a bowl & whisk together
with three half eggshells of cold water
Heat the butter and oil in a medium sized
non stick pan until foaming but not brown
Pour in the eggs & let them set for a minute
Add the goat cheese then gently drag the
liquid eggs from the edge back into the centre
until the frittata is done and the eggs are set
With a spatula loosen and slide out onto a
serving plate season with salt & pepper
Top with the herbs as many as you like
Finally drizzle over some more Olive Oil
Serve at once with sour dough bread
and butter

Following spread: I can't imagine life without my kitchen full of friends and family, who perch by the bench as we laugh, talk and cook.

La Dolce Vita

Italy

I love Italy as much as I love my home in Australia, but it's a different dance. Italy satisfies a hunger in me that Australia doesn't.

From Italy, I crave art and a heavily textured culture – there is a certain romance to that European way of life. When you think of Australia and Italy together, you see a lot of similarities and also a lot of contrasts. Where Australia is saturated in high-definition colour and an unyielding light. In Italy, there's a gentler hue. It's almost a degradation of light.

Everything has a patina. It's the pink tones of the terracotta and the muted green of ancient olive branches. It's paint peeling, it's a shimmer across ancient cobblestone, it's shadows swaying softly against rendered walls. There's a warmth and softness in the light.

When I think of Italy, I see its cities as embodying their own hues. In Rome, there's the subdued yellow of buildings and terracotta reds that illuminate with golden warmth. In Ostuni, Puglia, everything's so much whiter and shadows are a little sharper. In Venice, there's a spectrum of pale pink, rose and yellow. And Positano is a spray of vibrant bougainvillea and layers of sorbet-coloured buildings that taper down to the gemstone sea.

Italy is wistful and wonderfully romantic. It implores you to step into the love affair. It's there waiting, no imagination is needed, because in Italy, you may so easily live in a world of romance.

The Italian landscape is pock-marked with centuries of conflict and conviviality. The evolution is possible to see with your own eyes, from crumbling Roman ruins, to Moorish architecture in the south, and Greek inspiration everywhere.

People know the history of their country in Italy. They remember how populations were wiped out, they see how the sediment builds up, they've watched the procession of churches, religions, invaders and political regimes and they're still here, making pasta through it all. There's so much history that you can't even dream of condensing it, but you can follow the trail. A sense of a thread that brings you to the future. In some moments, in some places in Italy, the past is palpable.

You can step back and view the country in macro as you peer into the centuries that have gone before, but it's also beautifully micro. The minutia of everyday life is both whimsical and seductive. I love that the first thing people do in the morning is walk to get their coffee; there's a gradual opening up of daily life as the city wakes.

Rome, for instance, is unveiled from the night little-by-little and bathed in glorious light. Day follows in graceful sequences of ritual and routine. People talk about what they're having for lunch, and at lunch they talk about what they're having for dinner. Piazzas fill, then empty for siesta, before swelling again in the afternoon as everyone takes their 'passeggiata' or stroll. As dusk descends, an evening aperitivo rolls into dinner, followed by the click-clack over cobblestones as you walk home.

But no matter how far north or south you are, anywhere you go in Italy, the themes that govern life here are the same. Life is family, religion, food, art, and culture. I don't really know any other country that is all those things, all at once, and with so much sincere passion. There's a profound impact that religious culture has had for generations, and tied up with that is family, culture, music, art, but none of it is staged – it's just how life has always been lived here. Everyone tries to make life a party with good food, wine, friends, and family. I think that's what makes it such a romantic, wonderful place. It's why you never say goodbye to Italy – there are always plans to return. After all, no one wants to leave a good party.

I have lived in and loved many places in Italy and I can't see a time when I'd ever be prepared to bid it farewell – there is always a 'next time'. In the following pages you'll find vignettes from a life in Italy I love and the people whom are woven within it. There are moments captured in my Rome apartment, Arco del Monte, which we fondly call the 'piccolo penthouse'. It's a tiny, two-bedroom rooftop apartment and it looks like nothing from the outside, just crumbling paint and stone. But inside it's restored and bathed in beautiful light. It's charming and so close to the markets that we're able to easily join the cadence of Roman life.

Then there's my beloved Pugliese farmhouse, Casa Olivetta, which is almost 500 years old. It took many negotiations with Italian builders and three years to restore, but this labour of love has my heart. Here I relish calming walks in the beautiful grove of old olive and fig trees. In winter, everything is a sage-green watercolour – it's just mesmerising. I love the red, rich soil when you plough in spring and all the poppies come up in a scarlet carpet that contrasts against the white building and green olive trees – it's the colour of pizza. Also in spring, we pick baskets of wild asparagus and just eat them as we walk. It is 'la dolce vita' in every sense.

In this chapter, there are also frames from other Italian cities I cherish, such as the wonderfully chaotic Napoli and the grandeur of lesser-known Torino. And interspersed throughout are the creatives, co-conspirators and inspiring souls with whom I have connected over art, food and a love of Italy, and shared many meals with over the years.

Whether this ignites your own wanderlust for an Italian sojourn or recalls fond memories, I hope you enjoy the beauty that is this magnificent country and, perhaps, make a plan to re-join the party.

Piedmonte

I've been going to Torino (Turin) for about 20 years and, in my opinion, it's the greatest undiscovered city of Italy. Surrounded by the Alps, this grand city is in the Langhe area of Piedmont. Here, autumn is a gastronomic delight with the alba white truffle, porcini mushrooms and chestnuts all in season and wholly embraced. Paired with some of the finest nebbiolo, barolo and barbaresco wines that are produced in the region and plenty of great restaurants, Torino is a true food-lover's paradise. There's also an enormous amount of culture to discover in this city, from the beautiful Royal Palace with its elegant display of the finest royal china, to Torino's industrial importance as the home of Fiat, and its beloved football team, Juventus. I find it more sophisticated than Rome. While Rome has a frenetic energy, Torino is refined and gentle.

Torino

Opposite: Caffè Torino has been the meeting spot for politicians, poets and everyone else since 1903. They do an incredible Americano here.

I could spend all day poring over the books, posters and prints at Galleria Gilibert, a gorgeous antique bookstore in the city.

The café in the Royal Palace, Giadini Reali, is lined with a collection of the royals' elegant china and dinnerware.

They say the tramezzino (sandwich) was invented at Torino's famous Caffè Mulassano. Try the mascarpone and truffle sandwich served with a cremoso coffee.

Torino local and my wonderful friend, Mimi Thorisson, knows the best places to eat in the city.

The Galleria Subalpina is a divine renaissance revival building in the city, where a light-filled courtyard restaurant is edged with the most gorgeous boutiques.

Piedmonte

I met Mimi and her husband, Oddur, many years ago, we became very close friends and spent a lot of time together after lockdown in Italy. We're creative and adventurous, each with our own artistic bents. Mimi is an incredible cook and Oddur is a talented writer and photographer, who has an innate ability to capture moments that are both beautiful yet artfully dishevelled. We all seem to live in the moment and are passionate about similar things – family, friends, food, wine, art, music and dogs! It's why we all share a love for Italy and live with very few regrets.

Mimi & Oddur Thorisson

Whenever Mimi and I are together, talk always turns to food. This time, it's her wild borage ravioli, which she's making with her daughter, Gaia.

Mimi's wild Borage Ricotta and Pistachio Ravioli

1 Bunch of wild borage
1/2 cup grated parmesan plus extra for serving
200g Cows milk ricotta
Generous handful green pistachios
pinch nutmeg, 8 zucchini flowers
1 handful of fine semolina, 1 clove garlic
2 sage leaves, salt and pepper

Pasta dough - Place the flour with a pinch of salt on a board or bench and make a well in the centre. Add 3 eggs and initially mix with a fork then use your hands to bring it together. Start to knead with the heel of your hand, sprinkling the dough with additional flour if it feels too wet. Knead until it is soft and elastic but still slightly sticky, for 6 to 8 minutes shape into a ball & wrap in plastic wrap
Let it rest at room temperature for 30 minutes.

Borage filling for the Ravioli

Meanwhile make the filling. Wash the borage & dry in a salad spinner. Add to the bowl of a food processor along with parmesan, ricotta pistachios, nutmeg, salt and pepper
Blend until it makes a pleasing taste
You dont want to grind the nuts too fine, so they still have their texture
Taste and adjust seasoning
if needed.

Following spread: Enjoying dinner with Mimi and Oddur, two of their daughters, Audrey and Gaia, and, of course, their dogs, Humphri and Vita, at their home in Torino.

Making the Ravioli Parcels

Scatter flour over a large clean surface. With a rolling pin roll the dough out until it is just thin enough to fit through the rollers of a pasta machine. Roll pieces of the dough through each setting of a pasta machine until it is the thinnest it can be. Ideally have a young helper on hand to hold the pasta across their arms while you roll.

Cut the dough in half. On one sheet carefully scoop 1 tspn of stuffing for every 6-8 cm and then brush around each mound of filling with egg wash. Drape the second sheet of pasta over the first one gently pushing around each mound with your fingers to seal and remove any air bubbles. Trim each ravioli parcel with a sharp knife or PASTA ROTELLA to form a neat square. Line a baking sheet with waxed paper & scatter a good amount of semolina. Transfer the ravioli to the baking sheet Cover loosley with plastic wrap and place in the refrigerator

Pasta Sauce

Wash the zucchini flowers, dry on a teatowel & remove the stamens. Melt the butter in a pan together with the crushed garlic clove, then discard the garlic. Add the sage leaves & chopped zucchini flowers and cook through until brown and crispy. Season with salt & pepper To Serve Drop the ravioli into salted boiling water & stir gently. The ravioli is cooked when they float to the surface.

Scoop out with a slotted spoon and transfer to warm serving plates. Top with sauce & sprinkle with parmesan. Serve Immediatly.

Lazio

The eternal city of Roma has so many little moments that flutter together to form a whole dance. It's a lot like the murmurations of the starlings you can see from the rooftop of our apartment there. It's a magical, mesmerising motion that has no leader – it just swirls this way and that, and somehow makes a beautiful moving artwork. That's Roma. From the morning market to siesta and aperitivo, the city undulates through the day with a rhythm you can't help but be swept up in. Each day brings a new unexpected adventure. There is so much history to unearth, not just as you walk past archaeological ruins, but also set within the architecture, interiors and culture, such as the opera, the museums, myriad church domes and the eternal buzz of vespas. It's a city of shutters that never ceases to snatch my breath away.

Roma

Opposite: While locals somewhat unkindly call the Victor Emmanuel II monument the 'wedding cake', it has to be one of the city's most iconic buildings.

The Teatro dell'Opera di Roma is faded grandeur at its best. I love the patterns and shadows the light makes through the windows.

PIAZZA R.V

This is one of my favourite squares in Rome, it's a little oasis of birdsong tucked into the courtyard of the 15th-century Palazzo Venezia.

Roma

I fell in love with Andrea Ferolla's and Daria Reina's Rome store, Chez Dede, instantly upon discovery. They're both amazing collaborators and curators with a great sense of style, whom I met when I was guest editor for *Vogue Living*. Chez Dede is filled to the brim with fantastic pieces, from clothes to books, art and perfume. Andrea is the artist and Daria the photographer, they're great connectors and have a rotation of interesting creators who are hosted by the store throughout the year. Chez Dede is a must-visit when in Rome and I recommend going before noon, then crossing the road for lunch at Pierluigi.

Andrea Ferolla & Daria Reina

Following spread: Andrea Ferolla (left) and Daria Reina in their studio, which is attached to their store Chez Dede in Rome.

Capalbio

My friendship with Bonifacio Spinola was nurtured by his wife, Marina De Lagarda, whom we first met in Capalbio, Italy. He's a winemaker from Genoa, but also a benevolent soul and a great cook who is deeply passionate about his pesto – down to the size of the basil leaf. Marina is a painter and colourist and an equally fantastic cook. We've found this great, like-minded bond. When you go to a foreign land, you don't expect to find new friends, and suddenly, you're pleasantly surprised to meet wonderful people who become a part of your fold.

Bonifacio Spinola

Bonafacios pesto spaghetti

Traditional pesto is a blend of fresh basil garlic pine nuts extra virgin olive oil and Parmesan. I also add Pecorino Romano. It is important to source the smallest Basil leaves you can find so its not too bitter. The pinenuts are preferably the long variety from Italy or Turkey not short ones I prefer not too much garlic or it will overtake the other aromas

10g Pinenuts
½ clove garlic
50g Basil leaves
& extra for garnish

60g Parmesan grated
30g Pecorino Romano grated
Extra Virgin Olive oil
Salt & 300g dried Spaghetti

Use a food processor to pulse the pinenuts and garlic until finely chopped
Add the basil Parmesan and Pecorino & pulse again
Then with the blade running drizzle enough olive oil until it is just right not too liquid not too thick Add salt as you like it
Cook spaghetti until aldente
Drain, cool a little and put into a large serving bowl Mix in the pesto - you dont want the pasta too hot so it heats the pesto Garnish with more Basil Leaves - Serves 4

Bonifacio can talk at length about every detail of pesto, including the length and shape of the pine nuts and where they should come from.

Roma

Our 'piccolo penthouse' in Rome is nestled right in the city's beating heart, between Piazza Farnese and Campo de Fiori. We wanted to live in the historical centre to connect with the wonderful rhythm here and find our own routine within daily life. The apartment is very Roman in style with beautiful old tiles and a wonderful rooftop. We've filled it with old-world and contemporary Italian art and interesting pieces I sourced from antique markets around the city. It's close to the markets and our favourite cafes, bakeries and restaurants.

Arco del Monte

I was gifted this stone lion from an antiques dealer; it's one of many that were removed from the staircase at the old Roma Hotel.

I had this vanity carved by a stonemason from a block of marble. It's such a luxury in Italy to have these raw materials on-hand.

Every design decision in the apartment was about maximising space. It's small, but perfectly functional and beautiful. Lots of light makes a big difference.

Opposite: This artwork hanging behind my copper pots is by Bonifacio's wife, Marina De Lagarda.
Above: The view from our kitchen balcony is the very embodiment of Rome's wonderful patina.

Anchovy on Toast

Toast thin slices of Baguette

Spread with a generous amount of Butter then top with the Best anchovies you can find

Garnish with Roughly Chopped Parsley

My friend, Fiona Seres, is an Australian writer living in London. She loves food as much as I do, so we'll often cook together.

Peach and Mozzorella Basil Salad

4 white Peaches
1 fresh mozzorella
1 handful basil leaves
Extra Virgin olive oil
Caramelised balsamic vinega
salt and pepper

Slice the peaches and Mozzorella
and arrange on a platter
Make a dressing with olive oil, vinegar
salt and ground pepper
Garnish with basil leaves

Campania

Like most port cities in the world, Naples feels exciting and a bit dangerous – you have to negotiate the streets with care. There's so much history and many incredible museums, yet there is a sense the whole place is just crumbling around you. You never know what you'll encounter – there's wheelers and dealers everywhere, interspersed with nonnas making pasta and beautiful old churches. You can also find tucked-away speakeasies, great tailors and antique dealers here. Similar to India, Naploli has a chaotic energy, but there's also a calmness, if you know how to navigate it. This labyrinthine city is one of my most-loved in Italy, even for the food alone. It has three of my favourite restaurants, Mimi alla Ferrovia, Europeo Mattozzi (page 196) and Da Dora (opposite). Another highlight is the easy ferry access to the islands of Capri, Procida and Ischia and the proximity to the Amalfi Coast.

I always love visiting fish markets in any port city, and Napoli's is so vibrant and lively with the fish straight off the boats.

Opposite: Luigia from Ristorante Europeo Mattozzi will always welcome you with open arms. The Genovese ragu is a must-try!

Bellissima Colleen

grazie per amare così
tanto il nostro ristorante.
We love Australia and
you and Mimi.

Baci Francesca per
sempre
Madden 1971

Europeo Matozzi Genovese Ragu

500g veal leg cut into small pieces
600g Neapolitan golden onions chopped
Extra Virgin Olive Oil
~~salt~~
1 cup of Red Wine ☕
1 stalk of Rosemary 2 bay leaves
2 stalks celery chopped
3 carrots chopped
A few Piennolo Tomatoes or
1 tin tomatoes

Heat 3 tbsp olive oil in an ovenproof casserole dish (which has a lid) and cook the onions slowly.
When they are no longer watery add a generous pinch of salt, wine rosemary bay leaves carrot celery and tomatoes. Continue cooking so the ingredients are well combined into a sauce, Then add the veal.

Put the lid on the dish and place in the oven at 150° for 3 hours, checking if it has enough liquid.

Serve with long candle pasta broken by hand from Gragnano.

In Napoli some people use also mezzani or ziti.

Above: I love standing in an empty theatre, such as the Teatro di San Carlo, and pondering all the history and drama that has unfolded within.
Opposite: The ceiling dome is incredibly intricate; some of the greatest artworks in history can be found in these places.

The Gran Caffe Gambrinus overlooks Piazza del Plebiscito – it's somewhat touristy, but you can spend a happy afternoon here watching the world go by.

You can't turn a corner in Napoli without encountering a beautiful, old church, such as the Chiesa del Gesù Nuovo.

Designed to connect the nuns to the world outside, the Cloister of Santa Chiara is lined with incredible tiles depicting scenes of Napoli and beyond.

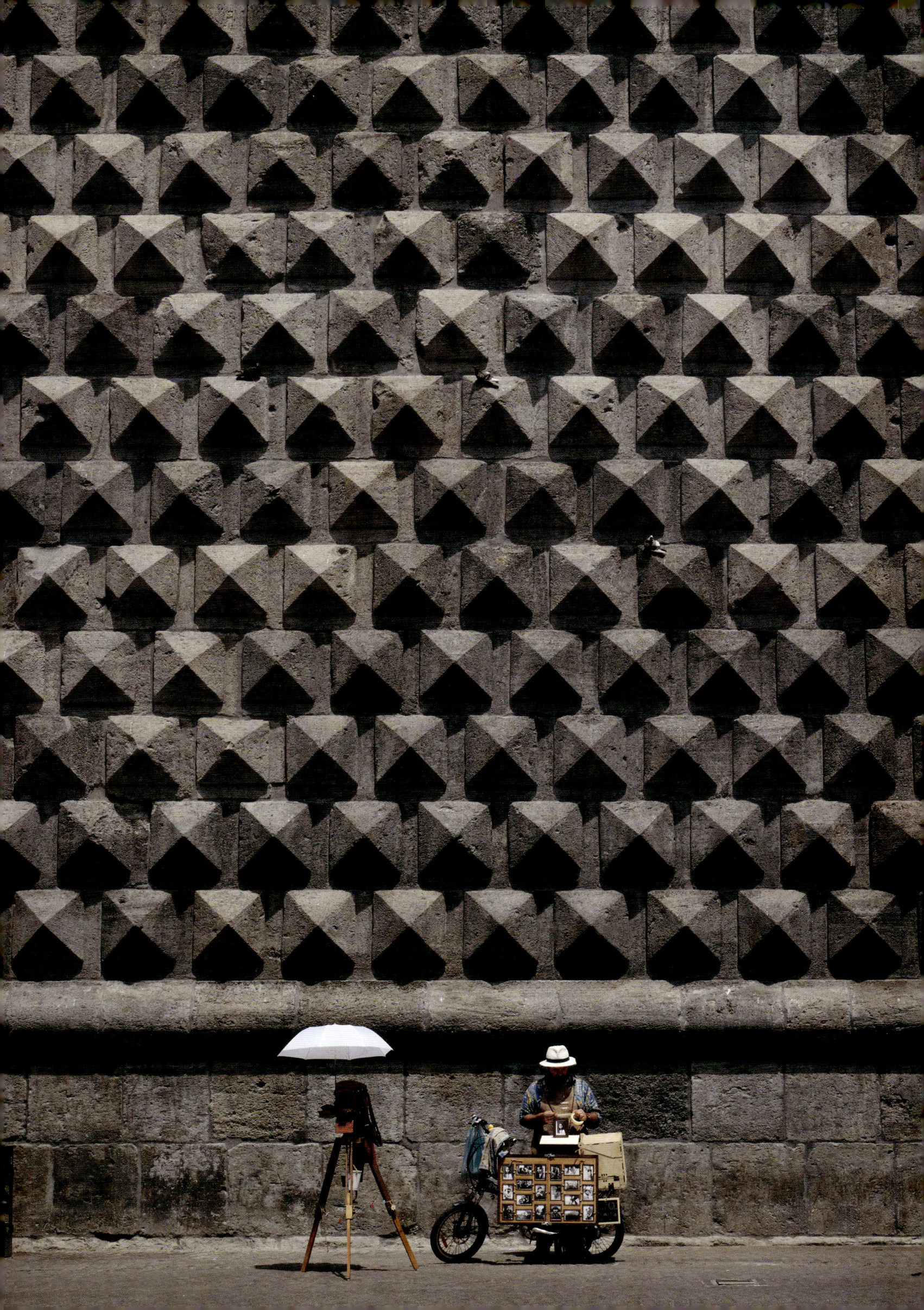

Bernalda

Folded into the hilltop town of Bernalda, Basilicata, Palazzo Margherita is owned by Francis Ford Coppola. It's a small, luxury hotel and a lovely, romantic snapshot of Italian life. I met Rosella De Filippo, the general manager (although she is way more than that) in 2017, when I was the guest editor at *Vogue Living* and we connected over food and ceramics. Her mother, Nina Silvestri, has taught me how to make orecchiette and Rosella has shared her famous lampascioni recipe on page 214.

Palazzo Margherita

Orecchiette Pasta

500g durum wheat
Semolina flour
2½ cups of flour

Put semolina flour on a wooden work surface
& create a whole in the centre like a volcano.
Gradually add water while kneading the
dough by hand until it achieves a smooth
consistency but not soft. Making & kneading the
dough isn't so difficult it just takes a little more
elbow grease than egg pasta dough.

Once you have made the dough and left
it to rest for a while, roll pieces of the dough
into 25cm sausages and then cut them into smaller
pieces (1-2cms). Using the rounded tip of a smooth
bladed knife, drag it across the board to create
Orecchiette.

You can make orecchiette any size you want
The important thing is that your pasta
is more or less the same size

Turn the pasta with your thumb
as needed for the desired shape

Rosella's mother, Nina, teaches me how to make the southern Italian specialty of orecchiette.

Orecchiette is an art form, but it's one you can quickly learn. For me, it has a rhythm that's akin to counting buttons.

Lampascioni with ficotto

A delicacy of Basilicata, Puglia and
Calabria, the lampascione is
the bulb of the wild tassle hyacinth
like an onion with a slightly bitter taste
Once the bulbs are harvested
trim the roots and outer
layers

Make vertical incisions into each bulb
without cutting through the base
Soak in cold water until they open out
Drain on a teatowel & then
fry in Olive Oil
till golden
Serve sprinkled with salt and
drizzled with ficotto
Caramelised fig syrup.

This haunting hilltop town is Craco, which was abandoned in the 1980s following a landslide. It's heartbreaking to see so many uninhabited villages around Italy.

Salento

When we first went to Puglia, it felt so undiscovered and wild. It captivated me immediately. The roads wind through a countryside that can feel barren and remote, then suddenly, you're in a valley surrounded by ancient olive trees and hillsides dotted with trullis. Each little town seems to sing its own melodic song. You can feel and taste the proximity to Greece and North Africa – once we even experienced a sand storm blowing across from Africa. The regional cuisine, which is referred to as 'cucina povera', meaning peasant cooking, is all about seasonal, local produce, such as sweet tomatoes, cima di rappa, artichokes, eggplants, garlic, anchovies, olives and, of course, olive oil. In summer, ancient fig trees are festooned with baubles of sweet, plump fruit just waiting to be picked. When here, make sure to visit the local antique markets and explore the naturally stunning grottos tucked into the coastline.

Puglia

The east coast of Puglia is dotted with grottos, but unlike Capri, they're not signposted, so you have to find your own way down.

Lo Scalo Ristorante is a favourite. I love that you can enjoy lobster spaghetti for lunch then dive off the rocks into the water below.

Opposite: A typical scene in Puglia is the top of a trullo popping above the trees.
Following spread: We pass this grand home on our way to Casa Olivetta. It's impossible to believe such an architectural treasure has been unoccupied for 100 years.

It all started with Rob Potter-Sanders. He is a conduit, a connector and the catalyst for us embarking on our journey in Puglia. His encouragement led us to purchase and restore our farmhouse, Casa Olivetta. He's a pioneer in the region and his hotel, Masseria Trapana, is a luxury destination. In Puglia, there is a community of like-minded people, such as Rob, who come from all corners of the globe and are attracted to the wild spirit of the region.

Rob Potter–Sanders

Ostuni

Katherine and I are two peas in a pod. We hit it off straight away because she's incredibly kind and loving towards the environment, nature and animals. She's an American-born interior designer with an innate sense of colour, but has spent most of her life in Italy since marrying into the Mondadori publishing family. She and her sister, Donna Price, live in the fabulous Masseria Lamacoppa, which sits on an estate full of protected cork trees, ancient olive groves, rescue dogs, donkeys and horses. Donna is the backbone of the operation that enables Katherine to keep this organic sanctuary for humans, animals and nature thriving.

Katherine Mondadori

Previous spread: Katherine (right) and her sister, Donna, in their formal living area, which is typical of the masseria style with its gorgeous vaulted star ceiling.

Masseria Lamacoppa is a series of beautifully decorated rooms with a mix of contemporary art and antiques, and an ode to North Africa.

The masseria is surrounded by olive and cork trees and is a sanctuary for all kinds of animals. Katherine has a great love of horses.

The internal courtyard is planted with lemon trees Katherine brought from her home in Capri. The scent of lemon after summer rain is intoxicating.

Above: The masseria's entryway provides a tranquil separation from the busy, pot-holed road beyond where Vespas and three-wheeled Apes buzz up and down.
Following spread: I've been lucky enough to swim in the beautiful Masseria Lamacoppa swimming pool, where you can swim to the spa through a canal.

Grottaglie

Grottaglie in Puglia has a long history of producing beautiful ceramics and Franco Fasano is a wonderful part of that tradition. The works made here, from urns to tiles and plates, are filled with an intent to create something everlasting and Franco is just one of the talented ceramicists that make up hundreds in the town. He is a man filled with colour, charm and calm, and he loves Australians. I have truly enjoyed collaborating with him on dinnerware from time to time.

Franco Fasano

Following spread: Franco enthusiastically welcomes everyone to his studio in Grottaglie, where I've had the pleasure of spending time decorating plates and enjoying his company.

Ostuni

This rustic, old farmhouse was one of the first we looked at in Puglia and, although we traipsed through countless more, we couldn't shake the belonging we felt to this charmingly rundown property. It took four years to nurse her back to her original beauty. I'd go down once a week from Rome to tussle with local tradesmen and plant vegetables. I had so much fun travelling to various art and antique markets around Italy sourcing old materials and furniture. The craftsmen were truly inspirational and it was such a great experience to work with them. Every effort was worth it to see this historic, 500-year-old home reclaim life anew.

Casa Olivetta

Previous spread: Our kitchen is where animals were once kept! Now there are two tables, one where we prepare food and the other laden with garden produce.
Above: Shirley from Masseria Lamacoppa is always smiling and ready to help. She's my go-to for traditional recipes, such as this fig galette.

Lamacoppa Fig Gallette

260g OO Flour
160g cold Butter
cut into 1 cm cubes
2 Egg Yolks
70g Castor Sugar. Zest of one
medium Lemon
1 small jar of home made Fig Jam
5 fresh figs sliced
A little brown sugar
A little Milk

You will need a 23cm fluted tart tin with a removeable base. Preheat the oven to 160° (fan forced) or 180° (no fan) Put flour on board or kitchen bench & make a well in the centre. Add the butter, egg yolks sugar & lemon zest Mix by hand until all the ingredients are incorporated. Divide the dough into 2 pieces, one 3/4 & the other 1/4
Press the large piece of dough into the fluted tin halfway up the side, making sure the dough is pressed well into the corner where the side meets the base. Spread Jam over the tart base Arrange figs over the layer of jam overlapping in a spiral pattern. Sprinkle with BROWN SUGAR.
Press the remaining ball of pastry out flat & cut strips with a knife to make an open Lattice pattern over the tart Brush the pastry with milk and sprinkle over a little more brown sugar. Bake for 35-40 minutes until pastry is cooked & tart is brown. Cool Remove from tin and Serve.

Tomato Salad

Slice perfectly vine ripened
tomatoes and sprinkle with a little
Flaky salt and pepper.
    Place on the platter
with fresh Basil leaves and
torn pieces or slices of Buffalo Mozzarella
Dress with Extra Virgin
    Olive Oil.

Whole Fish on a Platter

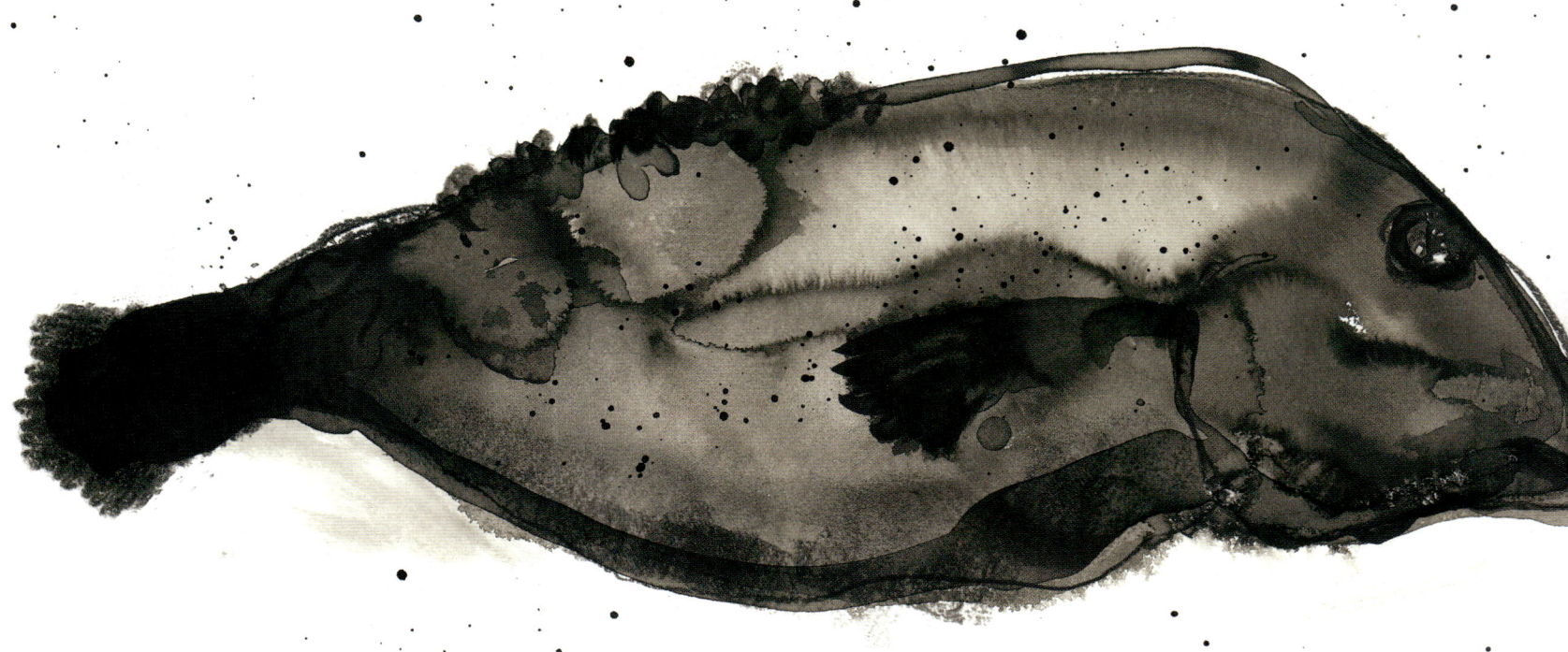

1 Sparkingly fresh Sea Bass of 3kg
gutted & scaled. 3 cups of green olives pitted
2 tbsp of capers in salt-rinsed
½ cup of chopped Italian Parsley
Extra Virgin Olive Oil & Pepper.

Preheat the oven to 200° Fill the fish
with olives capers slices of two lemons
parsley & ground pepper. Bake the fish on a
roasting dish with olive oil for 45 minutes
Serve with Lemon Wedges

Zucchini flower fritti

8 small to medium
zucchinis with flowers attached
¼ cup of plain flour
2 tbsp rice flour, pinch of bicarb soda
1 clove of garlic finely chopped
150 ml cold soda water
1 tbsp of Thyme or Sage leaves, chopped
olive oil, salt and lemon wedges to serve

Wash the zucchinis with their flowers and dry well
on a clean towel. Cut them in half lengthwise.
Remove the stamens from the flowers. Add the
flour, rice flour and bicarb soda to a bowl together
with garlic, herbs and one tbsp of olive oil
Mix ^ the soda water to make a smooth pouring
with consistency. Heat 1cm olive oil
in a fry pan until the test drop of batter
sizzles in a satisfying way.
Dip the zucchini in the batter
and fry till golden brown turning halfway
drain on a paper towel
Serve sprinkled with sea salt and lemon wedges.

Opposite: I love an entrance centrepiece, depending on the seasons I'll use ivy or grapevines. It looks beautiful at night with softly glowing candles.
Above: This enchanting, meandering pathway leads to the pool.

Above: These knights on horseback candlesticks are a traditional Pugliese ornament you'll find throughout the region; each is crafted to vary slightly in colour and shape.
Opposite: I fell in love with Casa Olivetta when I spotted these original red floor tiles. I had these blankets made to match them.

My love for collecting saw me travel as far as Milan, where I found this 1000-year-old, hand-carved basin that was once a wall fountain.

I kept all the nooks and crannies when renovating, as they make wonderful alcoves to display art and give a three-dimensional feeling.

Puglia has a very white colour palette with its lime-washed buildings, so I like bringing in contrast with dark wood and oil paintings.

Above: We built this separate guest cottage using beautiful reclaimed stone from an old masseria that was in ruins just outside of Lecce.
Opposite: I bought this antique bed frame from an antiques store called La Mercanteria in Ostuni, but I had other beds made by a local ironworker.

This pool is unconventional for Puglia with its raised sides. Locals thought I was crazy planting guara so close, but I don't mind a few petals.

I did all the planting and painting in this courtyard. The dry-stone walls are draped in rosemary, herbs and lemon balm, which keeps mosquitoes away.

We spend most of our time eating and escaping the summer heat under this pergola. At night the table is dressed with candles and wildflowers.

Punterelle Salad

1 Large bunch of Puntarelle
Juice of two Lemons
1 small tin best quality anchovies
1 clove of garlic
1 handful of grated parmesan olive oil & pepper

Puntarelle is one of the chicory family. The preparation takes time but is definitely worth it. Using a sharp paring knife cut away the bottom of the stalks & outer leaves (the outer leaves can be cooked in salted water and dressed in olive oil & capers to be served another time) Finely cut the top part of each inner stalk into strips and place in a bowl of iced water until they start to curl (about 45 minutes. Make the dressing in a blender with the lemon juice, anchovy fillets, garlic ⅓ cup of olive oil and cracked pepper.
Drain the puntarelle in a salad spinner, arrange in a bowl and spoon over the dressing

Following spread: Here you can see the original farmhouse (called a 'lamia') to the left and the new build to the right behind the 500-year-old olive tree.

Acknowledgments

To my husband, Bradley, and my children, Estella and Hunter –
you are the loves of my life. Thank you for always being there
and keeping the ground stable.

To Jason Siddons for never blinking an eye, no matter the challenge, and always being such a strong support across all my projects.

To the Puckeridge family, thank you for always being up for adventure and holding us to it – our trips and fishing expeditions are a true highlight. To Luke Sciberras, thank you for your talent, friendship, good food and for never saying no!

To Louise Olsen for being so patient, gentle, talented and a beautiful friend. Your ink illustrations are a stand-out, too. To Neil and Sam Perry, both such generous friends. Neil, your passion for food and its provenance is contagious. Like good wine, I think our vintage is only getting better with age.

To the Thorisson family, it is always a pleasure to be in your company. Thank you for allowing the lens into your home and for the wonderful and insightful tour of Torino.

Patricia Aldobrandini, thank you for opening your black book and introducing me to Opera Roma. Thank you Andrea Ferolla and Daria Reina from Chez Dede for such beauty and forever being the inspiring curators that you both are.

To Bonifacio Spinola, you are first and foremost a wonderful and generous human, as well as being a great cook and wine producer.

To Fiona Seres and all my other wonderful friends. The ones who love to cook and those who love to eat and help – our stories are a book in themselves. To Nikki Andrews, who always has the last word, because she cares and because she is usually right.

Thank you, Luigia from Europa Mattozzi in Napoli, for making lunch the most fun and for your Genovese ragu recipe. And to Rosella de Filippo for never losing the passion and to her mum, Nina, for being the most beautiful and glamorous nonna, who makes shaping orecchiette look effortless.

To Rob Potter-Sanders for telling us all as it is and still having a sense of humour. And to Franco Fasano, the ceramics king who has his arms and heart wide open to us all.

Katherine Mondadori, you have the love with style. Your support and help, no matter when or where, has been unwavering and generous. And Donna Price your humour and ability to keep it real makes me miss you always.

To Shirley for your generosity of spirit and delicious food.

Anna Johnson, it's never easy and so much work has been put into this publication, but each recipe is its own piece of art. Daniel O'Connell, your illustrations seem effortless, but they give fruit and vegetables a new kind of personality.

An enormous thank you to all the artists whose work fills our walls and gives our home so much beauty and personality.

To my photographer friends who always say yes and have contributed so much to my career. A huge thank you @felix_forest, @paulraeside and @hughstewart_ for also giving the last shots we couldn't capture but we have been on many a different ride.

Julie Gibbs you are the publisher of all publishers. Thank you for being such a warrior with a crystalline vision and a friend who stands unwaveringly by the creative souls whom you sometimes need to gently navigate.

To Vince Frost and Wing Lau at Frost*collective, there is so much talent between you both. It has been a pleasure and a privilege to work with you and your team.

Lara Picone for helping shape the words that I ponder over and for correcting the grammar my impatience doesn't keep up with. You have made what would have been rapids to me seem like a calmly flowing river.

To Earl, you win a big prize. What a pleasure to get to know you so much more and to share with you some of the wonderful storytelling from this book. Your pictures are pure beauty. Your capture of light is sublime and some of the moments in these pages are pure magic. I wish we didn't need to edit anything. Thank you for putting your heart and soul into this book. And thank you, Wanda, for getting Earl to where he is meant to be.

Last but never least, a huge thank you to Simon & Schuster for believing in this vision and making the commitment.

Ciao

Bellissima: An Australian—Italian Affair

First published in Australia in 2024 by
Simon & Schuster (Australia) Pty Limited
Suite 19A, Level 1, Building C, 450 Miller Street, Cammeray, NSW 2062

A JULIE GIBBS BOOK

for

SIMON & SCHUSTER
AUSTRALIA

10 9 8 7 6 5 4 3 2 1

Simon & Schuster: Celebrating 100 Years of Publishing in 2024
Sydney New York London Toronto New Delhi
Visit our website at www.simonandschuster.com.au

A catalogue record for this
book is available from the
National Library of Australia

ISBN: 9781761420344

Book design: Frost*collective/Vince Frost*/Wing Lau
Printed and bound in China by Asia Pacific Offset Limited

The paper this book is printed on is
certified against the Forest Stewardship
Council® Standards. Griffin Press holds
chain of custody certification SCS-
COC-001185. FSC® promotes
environmentally responsible, socially
beneficial and economically viable
management of the world's forests.

Illustrators
Anna Johnson (pages 165, 180)
Daniel O'Connell (pages 20, 27, 181, 195, 214, 261, 267)
Louise Olsen (pages 44, 83, 92, 262)
Luke Sciberras (pages 48, 51)

Calligrapher
Anna Johnson (all recipes)

Additional photographers
Felix Forest (pages 218–223; 228–229; 230–235)
Hugh Stewart (page 87)
Paul Raeside (page 224, 278)
Sam Armstrong (pages 48, 49, 51)

For more information, visit collettedinnigan.com